These Haunted Words
Jazmin Galloway

Copyright © 2022 by Jazmin Galloway

All rights reserved.

No portion of this book may be reproduced in any form without written permission from the publisher or author, except as permitted by U.S. copyright law.

Trigger Warnings
- ~Depression
- ~Mentions of suicide and self-harm
- ~Toxic relationships
- ~Sexual content

To all the ones who loved me.

HERE LIES THE WORDS of my latest creation.

IT WAS THE DEEP exhale
   of your sad heart
   that made me lose
   my self-control.

   Had I been
   another woman
   with different needs
   and the will to try,

   try I would
   for you
   because you made me sound sweet
   like liquid cane mixed in Kool-Aid.

   But I'm not
   a different woman,
   And you're stuck on the image of me

and what I mean
but not
who I am
in reality

I forgive you;

For overlooking my trauma
and the way it settled
into my dark eyes
that held your gaze.

For the nature of my tongue
   is flirtatious
   As you learn in dark rooms
   and cold nights.

   From memories of the past
   and imagery of the future.

   I am a facade beyond your wildest imagination.

   You will see
   that smoky words
   covered in roses
   are all I am.

   Even the most beautiful
   have thorns that prick.

COMPILATIONS OF COLOR
decorate the screen
beneath my thumb.

A world I've never known
begging to belong
to me.

If only I'd left the room
in the cast-iron cage
around my beating heart.

IF YOU WERE A ghost,
   you'd haunt me.
   But you're a man.

   Instead,
   your words
   are what keep me up at night,

   Watching the door
   to see if you'll enter
   my mind invasively
   to persuade me
   that I should die

   To be with you.

   Because we're much better together
   than apart.

That soil and worms
which rot your skin
should be in me
as well.

I AM TRULY A figment
 of your imagination.

 And the pigmentation
 of my skin
 is what blends me in
 to your backgrounds
 And saturates me
 in your foregrounds.

 My ill mind
 gives white lies
 and evasive answers.

 So you don't know much
 And you crave more.

 I don't know much

and I crave more.

Your soothing voice
   is like rain on concrete.

   The wet splatter
   and pitter-patter
   of emotional damage
   and mental fortitude.

   Balled together,
   weighed on my shoulders
   and heavy in my ears.

IT WAS NOT...
    the color of your eyes
    nor the smirk upon your lips
    that drew you to me.

    It was not...
    the looks or stares
    nor the snickers and whispers
    that drew you to me.

    It was...
    the silent plead,
    the desperate need
    to be seen,

    To be held,
    To divulge

in my intelligent mind
That drew you to me.

It was out of character
how quickly you fell
into my hands,

Then slipped away
like grains of sand,

Then through the floor
like phantom men

And disappeared
like rushing wind,

Never to be heard
or seen again.

I DID NOT MEAN
   to lead you astray
   nor display
   this massive chemistry
   that you convey
   as something more
   than what I portray
   at face value.

   I did not mean
   to let you like me
   as you do.

   Nor did I mean
   to let my words be hot
   and breathe on you.

   Or give you hope

to sip and chew.

How do I quiet these haunted words?

YOU DID NOT LOVE
  so quickly,

  But slowly,
  it did brew,

  And fill your warm words
  with lust I grew,

  And returned back
  so that you may track

  Through my imagery
  and illusive mind.

I CANNOT FORGET THE way you try,
   but I hold on to the way

   you give up
   and give in

   To the innocence that you crave
   and splay
   on those scuffed hardwood floors.

THESE SWEET WORDS
   may be my only exception
   to remembering you
   when you are gone,

   Immortalizing
   the feelings you gave
   when you fell for me.

   I ask of you
   to will for another woman,
   for I am no woman
   for you,
   And you are no man
   for me.

   We are only figments of a sleepless mind
   and shapeless dreams.

You've asked me questions
that I do not have the answer.

So, I give you this
as a way of saying
GOODBYE

To the man you once were,
because my poisonous words
kill.

They strike
and fill
and pull
and drill

Until you're thrilled
and lose your will

to hold on to hope
that change will come.

But rain will come
and I disappear
with the rising sun.

When you took my hand,
    I gave you all that you would get,
    A silent wish for you to forget,
    And one last look for you to remiss.

THERE IS BEAUTY IN the way
   these haunted words display.

   They lay and engrave
   what you should save

   In your heart
   until you start
   to foam at the mouth
   with begging words

   And the fish you caught
   leaves no worm.

I STILL FEEL THE *weight* of your hands around my throat...

I'm afraid you won't be gentle.

I still hear you asking what I mean.

I'm afraid you'll never understand.

I still think that you are too young.

No matter how small our age difference,

I'm still sorry that it was not meant to be

No matter how much you wanted it.

I KNOW YOU FEARED rejection
and stepped out of your skin to ask,
While I begged you not to speak
those words that you knew had no home.

There are some things I like
about the dog, the house, the tone.

The dog
Which never stops barking
and wagging its tail for its owner,
Nuzzled by the idea that together
means forever.

The house
Which so easily housed
the excuses of physical contact
When no contact was needed

to create a bond.

The tone
Which so easily
voiced an attraction to the mind
and not the body
Though the body was never ignored.

I AM NOT YOUR perfect woman,
    and your words describe me so.

    You are not my perfect man,
    but that knowledge hurts to know.

    Forget your insufferable encounter,
    and do not let these haunted words linger.

I HAVE THREE REASONS we did not work,
   Three reasons I do not wish to share,
   For all my reasons
   are broken records
   of words that have ensnared

   Inside your mind,
   embedded and shredded
   your self-confidence
   and stole your thunder.

   You still thunder to me,
   So, remain free
   of my three reasons,

   Or keep wondering
   and read on
   and remain haunted

forever long.

Reason number one

I asked if you wanted a child,
and it was too dark to see if you smiled.
But you said no at first, then changed your answer.
That raised all types of flags
not to enter
into a relationship
with someone who
couldn't find the answer in their limited truth.

And I would say I'm sorry,
But I'm really not.
The things we have in life,
we don't truly get.
Everything can fade
in the blink of an eye
or breath or second.

And what I want, I don't have.
So I use love as my weapon
to keep out the old
and bring the new.
Give everything I have
before it goes boom.

Reason number two

It's not a wage gap,
It's an age gap.
And that little bit of time
makes an impact
on my impressions
and my past transgressions
which are full of aggression
and mental depression.

You're not ready for what I want
and you know it well.
And while you're willing to try
and break free from your hell,

You're still a little too young for my maturity.
This was the intro to your purity.

I'm just a little too much spice covered in sugar,
And you're just a little too much water that turned to wine.
And since I don't drink,
it's time for me to go
and say goodbye
Cause I might have been a kiddo,
But I'm flying high.

Reason Number Three

I'd like to sugarcoat my words
in red velvet icing
so your brain will lick it up
and it will sound enticing.

But to be honest,
I don't have the energy
to make the blatant truth sound good
to you or me.

No matter how deeply you feel,
it doesn't change the fact
that what I look like wasn't your ideal
phat.
It isn't what you want
and I'm okay with that.

I just thought I should know before I did something
I couldn't take back.

In the vain of honesty,
I needed you to know
that I wasn't attracted to what you tried to show,

And that mutual discretion
is all I needed to know
That what was there wasn't more
than what we already sown.

There can't be much to salvage after a blow like that.
I'm fine with where we decided to be until you turned it back
  and threw it up
  and blew it out with a BB gun
  and stood pretty like it was sweet
  and not overdone.

"*Lust is a psychological force producing intense desire for something,*"

    For I lust after your attention
    But I did mention
    My intention
    and my dismissal
    of intervention
    in romance
    and other things?

    I always ask
    of future plans
    to see the man's
    values,
    Which I value
    and know the difference
    between going to work

and not.

We were not going to work
because my dreams
are different from yours.

"*HOPE IS AN OPTIMISTIC state of mind that is based on an expectation of positive outcomes...*"

I could feel your hope
in your energy,
which has an aqua color
that showed through
the murky black that covered
you

And
Smothered
You

And
Mothered
You

Into thinking
that this life
is not worth
the work you're putting in.

But it is,
you just can't see
what I see.

And that's for me to know
And you to find out.

But you won't know
if you leave too soon.

"*COMPLETE DISORDER AND CONFUSION*"

Chaos tastes so sweet
like nerds on a spring day,
surrounded by friends and family.

It devours and empowers,
and sucks away our towering
feelings,
And leaves us numb inside,

Like chewed gum
and empty bottles.

"*FREE OF DECEIT AND* **untruthfulness; sincere**"

Honesty
is hard to come by.
And I gave you all I could give
and all I was willing to.

When I turn off my over-thinking mind,
that's when I truly live.
And while my dismaying words
may make me sound like a brat,
I am okay with that.

For I like the young me
in which I play
the part
in your vivid daydreams.

"*ANY TYPE OF CHANGE that causes physical, emotional, or psychological strain*"

Stress
is the best type of love.

That pressure
that pushes
and fights for
more
type of love.

I want to push and fight
for that type of rub.
That pushing and tugging
all night
type of love, love.

But it's not with you,
and that stresses you out.
It's okay to punch around,
scream and shout,
but not with me.
I won't allow that
cause all that fighting is having
impact
on your mental.

And I'd hate myself
if that's all I was to you,
stressing your mental health.

"*THE FEELING OF A person who likes; fondness. a preference, inclination, or pleasure.*"

I don't know how you feel,
but I am sure you don't like
how it ended.

But I didn't end it.

I just told the truth,
Which you asked for.

I told you not to despise.
I asked if you were ready
for the whole truth
and not lies,
and you said yes.

And so I told you,
and it broke you
and rerolled you
into a ball
of all the things you hate about yourself
and all the things you hate about the world.
And now I feel guilty
about

These haunted words.

"*THE CHARACTERISTIC ATTITUDE OF mind or way of thinking of a person or group*"

Mentality
is the factuality of the environment
I was raised in.
And the people
who raised me,

A personification
of all that I am
bared nude
in front, like food
for all to consume.

I've grown tired of being eaten,
And hungry enough to feed
on the little compliments

and bigger needs
of those who need more care than they'll ever receive.

HAD YOU TOLD ME that you could tell
  I was lying,
  Maybe I wouldn't have tried so hard
  to hide who I was, and fight what I wanted
  from you.

  I was hurt when you said your desire of me was little
  but your infatuation was large.

  I want to be desired by those haunted words,
  but instead, I am ridiculed

  I know attraction works both ways,
  But I am not averse to improvement.

  You leave room for improvement.

HAD I NOT LIKED something about you,
    your words would not have become my own,
    dripped from the tips of my fingers
    into my keyboard,
    and shocking the tops of my thighs
    down to my bones
    as I write to the image of you I've dreamed up,
    and not the real you
    who exists so far out of reach of everything
    I've dreamed up.

I'M SICK TO THE stomach,
   thinking of what-ifs,
   That my truth
   becomes your lifeline.
   And when I lie,
   it snaps
   and breaks,
   and you fall
   into a vat
   of darkness
   you can't get out.
   And you die there,
   cold and alone.

But, I give myself too much credit.
I don't mean as heavily as I think I do,
But your words don't convince me of that
and I feel sick again,

Guilt heavy on my consciousness.

SOMETIMES I REMEMBER
   that love is
   too powerful,
   too scary,
   and too hard to control.

   And I rather not get myself
   into another situation
   out of my league.

I HAVE A ROUGH understanding of what you want from me;
A symphony of ohs and ahs,
and pure honesty.

A rush of exhilarating banter
and fluttering lashes
with soft words and softer splatter
of you and me
mixing in the bed of your mind.
In mine
or yours,
it doesn't matter.

But I've already dug my grave and laid in it.
Reborn again
From the self-love I practiced.

I've no time to go backwards

and eat the shit I preach,
I can only go forward
and reach for peace.

You've praised my mentality,
   eyes, and smile.
   It's only a matter of time before you imagine a child,
   A creation of you and me.
   It doesn't have to be physical,
   But one for you to teach,
   nurture it and let it grow.
   When acid rain falls,
   it melts like snow.

And I've asked it before,
So, I'll ask again;
How do I rid these haunted words
for which I sin?

Exit my mind
   stage left

                                              Write my heart
                                                    stage right

                    Even if you start
                    CENTER STAGE

There will always be missed directions
Front page
of the news

It's my breaking point

With you on that platform,
you might break a joint.

But you're happy to take the plunge
And I admire that.

But not everything that you break
can be wrapped.

You're dancing to the tunes,
   and you walk the plank.

   Falling into my misery,
   you might take a drink.

   Eating all my history,
   you might stop and choke.

   All of my words,
   you may think a joke.

   But all of these feelings,
   can't be revoked.

   I may not have liked you affectionately,
   But what we had was special to me.

It was an instant bond, platonically,
and I hope we remain friends symbolically.

HAD I KNOWN I was special,
    I would have acted as such.
    Rendered speechless by your words,
    I couldn't say much

    Misunderstanding the effect
    I had on you,
    Minimizing the neglect
    that you accrued,

    In lieu
    of all that you are,
    all that you know,

    Here lies your haunting
    words,

    *So that they may **glow**.*

MAY THESE HAUNTED WORDS rest in peace.

Limpid Series
Black Or With Sugar?
Windchimes and Sirens
Murder Bird
Light and Sweet

Poetry Collections
Larceny
Mournful Lover

JAZMIN GALLOWAY started writing poetry in the third grade. With decades of practice came many life changes, achievements, losses, and mistakes. Galloway uses her life experiences and dreams of life to come, and life that has passed, to inspire her poetry. You can find her on Facebook and Instagram @jazminsbooks

www.ingramcontent.com/pod-product-compliance
Lightning Source LLC
Chambersburg PA
CBHW052206070526
44585CB00017B/2089